*This Space is the property of* **HILLMAN AND HERBERT, PREMIER WORKS, COVENTRY,** *who have already so many Orders on hand for their New Patent* **D H F** *that they dare not use it for advertising purposes, fearing it would secure further Orders, which they would be unable to execute as quickly as required.*

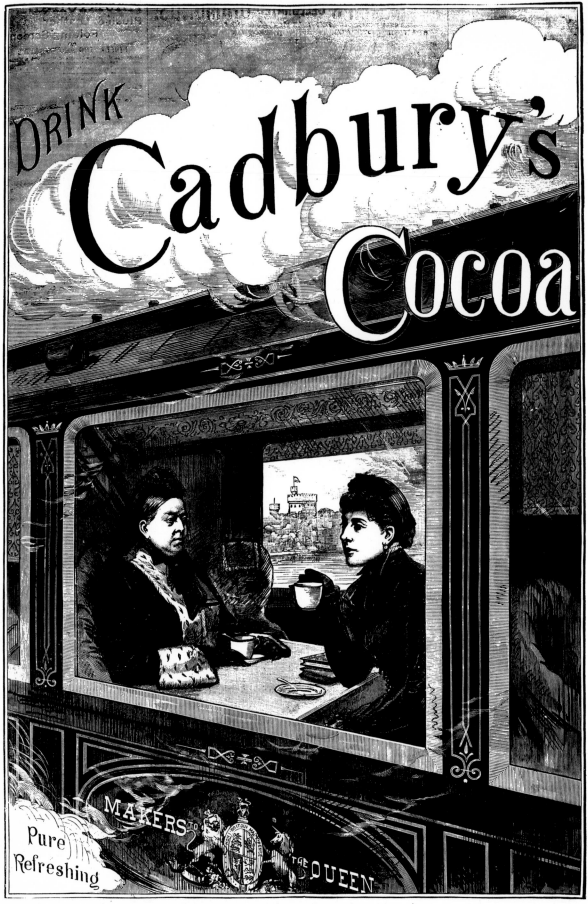

DRINK Cadbury's Cocoa

Pure Refreshing

MAKERS TO THE QUEEN

CAUTION.—Imitations of Cadbury's Cocoa are often pushed by Shopkeepers for the sake of extra profit. Be sure that you obtain the Original Article, which may be relied upon for excellence of quality, purity, and strength.

PARIS DEPÔT: 90, FAUBOURG ST. HONORÉ.

*Leonard de Vries*

# VICTORIAN ADVERTISEMENTS

Compiled in collaboration with Ilonka van Amstel

from the collections of Mr. Roland Knaster

and the British Museum

TEXT BY JAMES LAVER

*J. B. Lippincott Company, Philadelphia & New York*

# ACKNOWLEDGEMENTS

I am grateful to Mr. Roland Knaster whose albums of advertisements provided the first stimulant; to the Staff of the British Museum at Colindale for their enthusiastic and valuable help; and to Mr. James Laver for his co-operation.

L. de V.

# CONTENTS

*For Index of Sources see p. 134*

Advertising is as old as Humanity: indeed, much older; for what are the flaunting colours of the flowers but so many invitations to the bees to come and 'buy our product'. Everything is already there: the striking forms, the brilliant hues, even the 'conditioning of the customer'. One can almost see 'personal shoppers only' inscribed at the entrance to the calyx. But, in human terms, advertising might be defined as any device which first arrests the attention of the passer-by and then induces him to accept a mutually advantageous exchange.

In its most primitive form advertising is merely an announcement that somebody has something to sell: a bush outside the hut of a vigneron, a phallus scratched on the wall of a house in Pompeii, an inscription in chalk or charcoal beside the door of Greek theatre or Roman circus. When paper came into use the inscription would be written on that, and affixed to wall or post—which, incidentally, is the original meaning of the word poster: something stuck on a post.

The Romans had even discovered the hoarding, for in the ruins of Herculaneum was discovered a wall divided by pilasters into panels and on these were announcements in red and black paint of gladiatorial combats and other attractions. The names of the principals were displayed in large letters, and there were pictures too, for Pliny mentions a certain Callades who excelled at this kind of painting.

Lettered posters, of course, imply the existence of a literate public. When this was lacking, as in the Middle Ages, the poster gave place to the cryer. Posters did not appear again until the end of the fifteenth century and they seem to have been used at first for political purposes. With the invention of printing they proliferated and governments were compelled to enact stringent laws to govern their use. Official posters, for example royal proclamations, were the first to use pictures, usually merely the royal arms. Recruiting posters were embellished with woodcuts, sometimes coloured by hand and, in the early years of the eighteenth century, troupes of acrobats began to make use of the same device. Examples have survived and are now preserved in the *Cabinet des Estampes* in Paris.

The advantage of woodcut was that, being a relief process, it could be printed with the type in a single operation. With the intaglio processes such as engraving on copper this was not possible, but large numbers of trade cards of the late eighteenth century have survived exploiting the delicate line of the burin to great advantage. They were particularly popular with silversmiths who were thus able to offer an advertisement of their wares and a specimen of their craftsmanship at the same time.

Woodcut was, by its nature, somewhat crude in its technique, and it was a great advance when, in the early nineteenth century the process of lithography was discovered. The true pictorial poster was now possible but it remained obstinately monochrome until half way through the century. Then, in England, experiments began to be made of printing lithographs from several stones, a different coloured ink being used on each. The results were used to advertise the melodramas so popular at the period. The drawing was crudely realistic and the colours blatant but technically such posters marked a real advance.

And then came Jules Chéret who learned his craft in England and, returning to France, began to produce posters from much larger stones, and marked, it is hardly necessary to say, by a much higher standard of artistic merit. From 1867, when he designed a poster for Sarah Bernhardt, to the end of the century he produced nearly a thousand posters, nearly all for theatres or music halls, the Folies-Bergère or the Moulin Rouge. He was followed by Toulouse-Lautrec, the greatest poster artist of all time.

Meanwhile advertising had spread to other media of communication: the newspapers and magazines. Even in the eighteenth century newspapers had carried rather timid little announcements of goods for sale. What transformed the situation was the rise of pictorial journalism in the 1840's. Most of the illustrations were in woodcut, or rather wood-engraving, for the level of craftsmanship had risen sharply with the use of small squares of hard box-wood screwed together. A fine line was now possible, and indeed some of the blocks in a magazine like *The Illustrated London News* are miracles of technical skill.

Advertisers, however, were still fumbling in the dark. Some of them thought that mere repetition was enough, and that it helped to sell their product if they simply printed its name over and over again on the same page. Repetition is, of course, a very important element in advertising but not, perhaps, in this primitive form. A mere announcement, however often repeated, is not enough. It is necessary to catch the eye and this can most easily be done by some striking image, coupled if possible with an arresting slogan: a monkey in evening dress holding up a shining immaculate frying pan, and, in large letters over his head: 'Monkey Brand Won't Wash Clothes'. This 'negative approach' is still a potent weapon in the advertiser's armoury.

We can trace the beginnings of a more penetrating psychology in the 'Before and After' advertisements so popular in the last quarter of the nineteenth century: a picture of a wretched creature who has not yet taken *our* pill, and the same transformed into heroic manhood after he has taken it. Or a picture of a woman on the left with long, lank hair who has not yet tumbled to the fact that with the aid of *our* curlers she can transform herself into the kind of professional beauty depicted on the right.

Snob-appeal was already beginning to raise its enticing head, and some of it was of a blatancy which would hardly be permitted today. In the 1870's tailor's advertisements almost invariably show the head of some prominent politician, or even of some Royal Personage stuck on the top of a tailor's dummy. Did they mind? We have no record of any prosecution. Was Mr. Gladstone distressed when he was depicted as chopping down trees while wearing an Electropathic Belt? And what of the advertisement which showed him presiding over a Cabinet meeting with every member of the Cabinet named, and all singing the praises of one particular brand of tea? Pope Leo XIII can't have been exactly pleased to find himself linked with Bovril as one of the 'Two Infallible Powers', and wasn't it lèse-majesté to suggest that when the Prince of Wales met the Shah of Persia their conversation was entirely concerned with the superior quality of Bushmills Whisky?

Part of the value of the present compilation is as a footnote to history. For the social historian of the later Victorian period it offers a veritable mine of information, both in the field of technological advance and of moral climate. How soon, for example, was it possible for an advertiser to show a picture of a woman in her under-clothes or in a corset? Such pictures would never have been allowed in the editorial pages of a magazine, but they gradually made their way into the advertising sections.

In the technological sphere all kinds of novelties were being introduced: the 'penny-farthing' and, later, the 'safety' bicycle, the primitive motor-car; a waterproof 'free from odour' (the earlier oilskins stank like a pole-cat); the first refrigerator, called a 'self-feeding Ice Safe', making it unnecessary to buy 'Original Blocks of ice from High Lakes, Christiania, Norway' at 7/6d. per cwt.; primitive roller-skates, revolving heels ('the Most Useful Invention of the Victorian Era') and a phonograph 'Loud as a Man Sings'. There was also an Improved Atmospheric Churn—'Butter in Five Minutes', and the 'Registered Tourist's Bath which combines the advantages of a travelling trunk, foot, nursery, sponge, and hip baths'—just the thing, perhaps, for 'wintering in Egypt' or moving up to Simla in the Indian summer. It is not a bad thing that we should be reminded of the sheer discomfort of some aspects of Victorian life.

We can congratulate ourselves a little also on an in-crease in sensitivity. We no longer think it funny to contemplate an advertisement, 'Bovril by Electrocu-tion', showing two wretched animals tied up in the electric chair. It would, I think, be unlikely to induce us to buy the resultant product.

Another striking change is in the accepted ideal of feminine beauty. There are few slimming advertise-ments but we find plenty informing us that Cadbury's Cocoa is composed of 'Flesh Forming Ingredients', or recommending various methods of increasing the size of the bust. Flat-chestedness was indeed regarded as one of the greatest possible misfortunes. What we would now consider as a very well-formed girl is shown as utterly neglected while all the gentlemen pay court to a prima

donna-like lady with a bosom like the figure-head of a ship. There has been a real change here in the erotic-aesthetic.

And of course the advertisements themselves have improved—if improvement it be. What strikes us about Victorian publicity is its comparative naïvety—its lack of psychological understanding. Freud had hardly yet been heard of, and no-one had tumbled to the idea that 'sex will sell anything'. Our advertisers have become much cleverer; in fact, as some might think, too clever by half. Chesterton, more than a generation ago, was pointing out the dangerous element in the new tech-niques and, since his day, the power of advertising has increased a hundred-fold. The Devil's progress would seem to be: Advertiser—Public Relations Officer—Minister of Propaganda—Big Brother.

With the development of 'motivational research', advertising, as one of its leading practitioners proudly asserts, uses 'the modern techniques of social science and the interviewing techniques developed in clinical psy-chology and psychiatry'. The buying public is indeed stretched upon the psychiatrist's couch, and (it no longer surprises us to learn) most of its motivations boil down to sex! The writer we have already quoted declares that 'we discovered that tractors and steam shovels take on sexual characteristics when filtered through the engineer's emotions. One recalls such terms as "male" and "female" applied to nuts and bolts'. All this is more than a little alarming. And then Mr. Vance Packard comes along with his *Hidden Persuaders* to terrify the life out of all of us.

Propaganda indeed is the new Magic. It does not operate on the plane of the conscious intelligence. No-one was ever converted by its arguments; in fact it hardly proceeds by arguments at all. It deals in affirma-tions, repeated until their effect is hypnotic. It deals in suggestions aimed at the weakest link in the victims' armour; and the weakest link is where the conscious and the unconscious join. A slogan is a spell of words; a party badge or a trade symbol, a magical emblem. Propaganda, like Magic, is an assault on the psyche of others.

There is a sense, of course, in which advertising pays for itself. Every daily paper we buy is subsidized by the advertisers without whose help we would pay not pennies but shillings for each copy. What the advertisers themselves get out of it we must leave to the pundits of 'consumer research'. Perhaps there is such a thing as counter-productivity in these matters. Like the rabbits may we not be developing a certain immunity?

These are deep matters and part of the charm of the present compilation is its comparative innocence. The practitioner is still no more than an *apprenti sorcier*, and we find him as amusing as a little boy performing con-juring tricks. We have an uneasy and growing suspicion that the clever little advertising boys of today are not manipulating rabbits; they are manipulating *us*.

The Victorians were much concerned with their health, as well they might be. When we look at the menus of the meals they ate every day we can only stand amazed that the human frame could endure such an intake of proteins, such an avalanche of carbo-hydrates. No wonder they needed California Syrup of Figs, not to mention the unbeatable panaceas: Beecham's Pills and Eno's Fruit Salt. They cured their dyspepsia with Vogeler's Curative Compound, and hastened their convalescence with Mariani Wine (strongly recommended by the Pope himself).

They also took a lot of violent (indoor) exercise. A surprising number of advertisements in this section are concerned with various mechanical means of exercising the muscles, although some of the machines were so bulky and elaborate that only in a large house could room have been found for them. Side-whiskered gentlemen still wearing their frock coats and fancy waistcoats lean their ample 'corporations' against contraptions that massage and pummel them. Some bestride a mechanical horse which 'invigorates the system by bringing all the vital organs into inspiriting action and . . . prevents stagnation of the liver'. The 'family gymnasium' might also include a 'rowing apparatus' and, of course, a Turko-Russian Folding Bath Cabinet which cured 'colds, pneumonia, gout, rheumatism and nervous diseases.'

Pseudo-science began to play the part it still plays in therapeutic advertising. Electric light was, by the end of the century, being installed in theatres and restaurants and in some private houses. To what other uses could the magnetic fluid be put? Electricity was the new magic and all kinds of quarters began to exploit its possibilities—and impossibilities. The Medical Battery Company Limited, of Oxford Street, assured the public that its Electropathic Belt had 'restored thousands of sufferers to health and vigour', and had 'proved an inestimable blessing to the weak and languid'. It was particularly recommended for 'weak men suffering from the effect of youthful errors'. Did the weak men in question wear the contraption in bed? Women also could benefit by it, and one is a little surprised to find this and other remedies for 'female irregularities' so frankly discussed. An Electric Corset was the 'Very Thing' for ladies. One can only wonder how the batteries—if there were any—operated. And what could possibly be meant by an 'electric' towel, and how could failing sight be cured by an 'eye battery'?

The Victorians suffered much from bad teeth, and dentistry was in a surprisingly primitive stage. As late as 1890 a dentist could proudly claim that his teeth could *also* 'be used for purposes of mastication'. Most of those sold seem merely to have been clipped on for the purpose of smiling. There seems to have been quite a market in *second-hand* false teeth.

Corns were another problem due to the tight boots of the period, but Bond's Marvellous Corn Cure gave 'immediate relief from pain, and in a few days removes Bunions, Corns, Warts, Chilblains, Swellings etc.' Condy's Fluid was recommended for 'tender feet'.

The value of cleanliness was beginning to be appreciated, and all kinds of patent soaps claimed special properties. Pears' was of course the favourite ever since the firm's brilliant stroke of buying the painting of 'Bubbles' from Sir John Everett Millais. It was 'recommended for the complexion by Madame Adeline Patti and Mrs. Langtry'. The same soap, it seemed, could wash little negro boys white; and there were two pictures, 'Before' and 'After' to prove it. No-one would dare to print such an advertisement today.

The Victorians had plenty of soap: what they lacked was a ready supply of hot water. Hence the extraordinary geyser-contraptions which began to appear in advertisements. Hence, too, the class distinction implied by standards of cleanliness. The upper classes could still joke, as they had done in Dickens' day, about 'the Great Unwashed', meaning those whose standards of cleanliness were—inevitably—lower than their own. Such cleanliness was achieved by what can only be described as slave labour—the wretched housemaids who had to fill and empty all the hip baths. 'Constant Hot Water' as well as 'Central Heating' were still far in the future.

## THE FORMULA OF BRITISH CONQUEST

### PEARS' SOAP IN THE SOUDAN.

"Even if our invasion of the Soudan has done nothing else it has at any rate left the Arab something to puzzle his fuzzy head over, for the legend **PEARS' SOAP IS THE BEST,** inscribed in huge white characters on the rock which marks the farthest point of our advance towards Berber, will tax all the wits of the Dervishes of the Desert to translate."—Phil Robinson, *War Correspondent (in the Soudan) of the Daily Telegraph in London,* 1884.

---

---

---

---

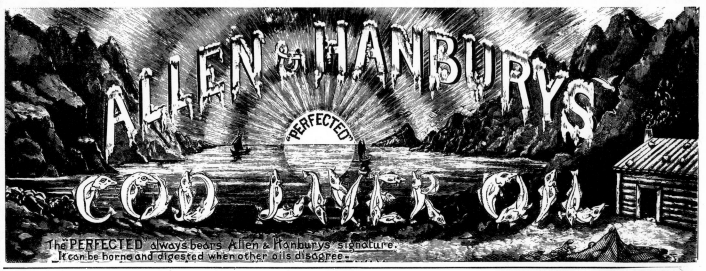

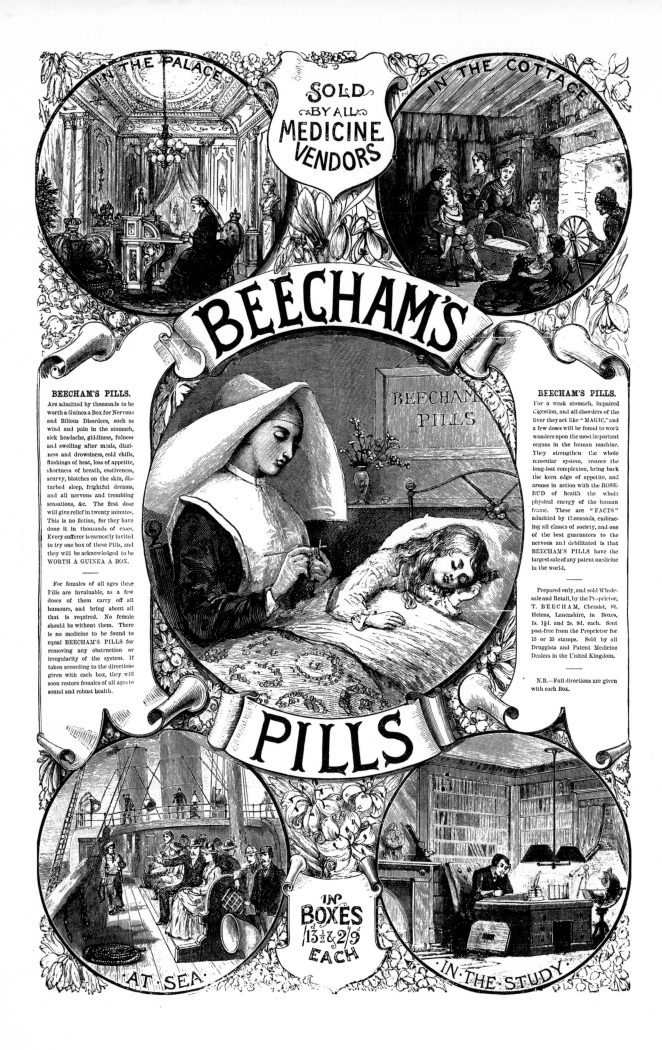

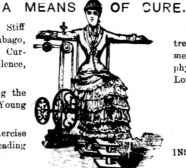
15

# PEARS' SOAP

## a Specialty for Children

WITH THE GUARD.　　WITHOUT THE GUARD.

"JUST WHAT'S WANTED."

## THE NEW (Registered.) FOOD GUARD.

A Most Useful and Welcome Help for
**Young Children Learning to Feed Themselves.**

Prevents the food being pushed over-edge of plate on to the table cloths; prevents soiling carpets and table linen; helps the child to fill its spoon easily. Is very simple, and can be fixed or removed (from any medium-sized plate) in a moment.

Strongly plated and free by post, 30 stamps, or P.O.O.

**FRANCIS E. SPILLER,** Silversmith & Cutler,

71, NEWINGTON CAUSEWAY, LONDON.

---

## PARRISH'S "GOLD MEDAL"

"*Strengthens children.*"

## CHEMICAL FOOD.

The *only* Chemical Food ever recognised by an INTERNATIONAL JURY of medical men, and awarded a Gold Medal for Excellence. Sold only in our ¼lb. and 1lb. bottles, **10d.** and **1/3** each.

**Caution.**—See that it bears the name **Parrish's "Gold Medal" Chemical Food,** also our name and trade-mark, and avoid all imitations.

Do not give your child inferior substitutes.

Sole Proprietors:

## LORIMER & Co.,

**Britannia Row,**
London, N.

Estab. quarter of a century.

---

## A THOROUGH TURKISH HOT AIR AND VAPOUR BATH FOR 3d.

ALLEN and SON'S is acknowledged to be the BEST BATH yet introduced for simplicity, cheapness, and thorough efficiency.

By its construction will generate a larger amount of hot air or vapour, separate or combined, than any other portable apparatus. Can be used for every purpose of general or local application, applied to bed, or used under a chair, &c. Price, complete, packed in case, 30s.

Inventors and Manufacturers, JAMES ALLEN and SON, 64 and 65, Marylebone-lane, London, W.

---

## BABY CARE TAKER & EXERCISER,

INVALUABLE where there is a BABY.— A useful purchase. A welcome present. Folds into small compass; is perfectly portable; requires no securing. Is perfectly firm; cannot be thrown over by the child. Is a constant source of interest and amusement to the baby. For use in any room—the lawn—the sands, &c. Thoroughly substantial; very handsome. Price, handsomely japanned, 35s.; superior in brass, 55s. Free of charge for packing for P.O.O. cheque, or reference.—S. FAWCKNER, NICHOLLS, and Co., Manufacturers, 35, Bridge-street, Bristol. London Agents: R. FISHER, 188, Strand; MEAD and Co, 73, Cheapside.

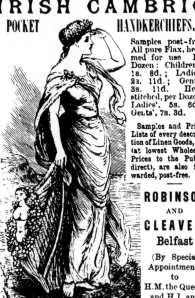

# BOVRIL by ELECTROCUTION

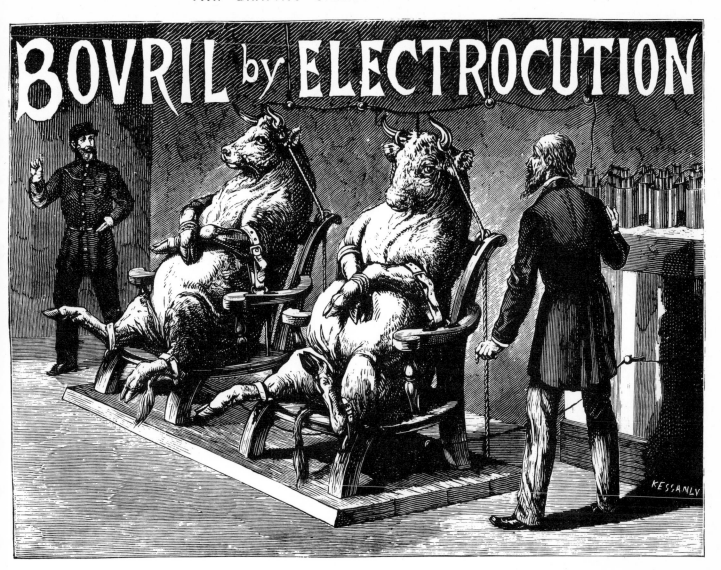

23

"Of absolute purity and freedom from alkali, Cadbury's Cocoa may be prescribed without hesitation with the certainty of obtaining uniform and gratifying results."—*Braithwaite's Retrospect of Medicine.*

FLESH FORMING INGREDIENTS.

In every 100 parts of Cocoa.

| | |
|---|---|
| Cadbury's Cocoa Essence | 34¾ |
| Best French Chocolates | 11 |
| Best Homœpathic Cocoas | 13 |
| Cocoa Nibs | 23 |
| Dried Milk | 35 |

*Cadbury's Cocoa, being the strongest in Flesh Formers and Absolutely Pure is therefore the Best Cocoa.*

---

For improving & preserving the complexion.

Pears' Soap.

Sold everywhere.
unscented tablets
6ᵈ each.
larger tablets
scented
1/- each.

Recommended for the complexion.
by Madame Adelina Patti & Mʳˢ Langtry.

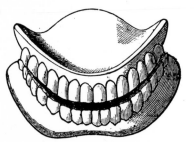

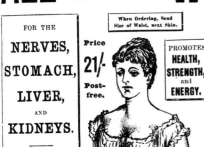

*Exercise is as essential to bodily development as air is to life.*

## HARRISON'S PATENT ROWING APPARATUS & FAMILY GYMNASIUM

Affords harmonious and simultaneous exercise to the whole body. It is rowing in the room with the advantage of rowing on the water, the Tension Bands affording a capital illustration of the "resistance" of water. The sliding seat and every detail of rowing is observed, and all the benefits of the exercise realised.

A slight change converts the machine into a **Health Lift**, and to fifteen other different exercises, thus forming a **complete Gymnasium**. For Training it is invaluable either for **Rowing, Cricketing, Football, Bicycling,** or any other athletic exercise, as it can be used when it is impossible to obtain training otherwise. Its use corrects the rounding of the shoulder and contraction of the chest, which Bicycling has a tendency to cause, and at the same time brings harmoniously into play the other muscles not developed by this exercise.

Price of Apparatus, in case complete, £2 2s.

Agents—F. S. PEAKE, 22 Wardour St.; and GOY & CO., 21 Leadenhall Street.

# MOUSON'S
# COCOA BUTTER SOAP
### (SAVON AU BEURRE DE CACAO).

This celebrated Soap consists chiefly of Cocoa Butter (extracted in the manufacture of Chocolate), which is the mildest fat known, and possesses a wonderfully healing and softening influence upon the skin. The beneficent and soothing properties of this product make themselves apparent by the delicious creamy lather it produces, rendering even the coarsest skin as soft as velvet. Cocoa Butter Soap is a real skin beautifier, and a balm to old and young alike.

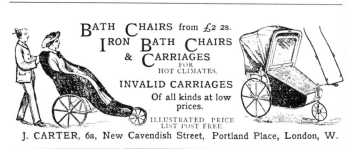

29

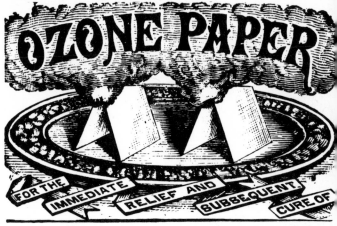

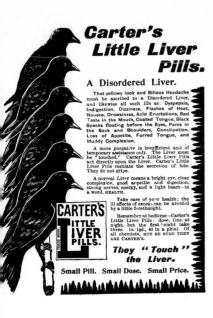

# HORSE EXERCISE AT HOME.

By Royal Letters Patent

## Vigor's Horse-Action Saddle

TROT, CANTER, & GALLOP.

VIGOR LONDON

The *ADVANTAGES* of this *UNIQUE SUBSTITUTE* for Horse-Riding are:

It promotes health in the same degree that Horse-Riding does.

It invigorates the system by bringing all the **VITAL ORGANS** into **INSPIRITING ACTION.**

It acts directly upon the **CIRCULATION,** and prevents **STAGNATION OF THE LIVER.**

It is a complete cure for **OBESITY, HYSTERIA,** and **GOUT.**

**PARTICULARS, TESTIMONIALS, and PRESS OPINIONS POST FREE.**

## Vigor & Co. 21, Baker St., London.

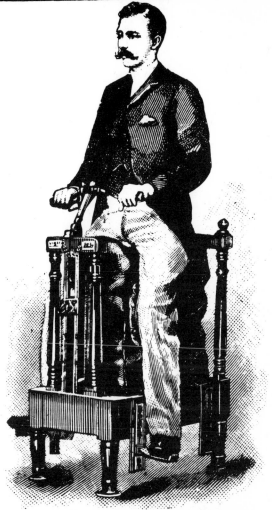
33

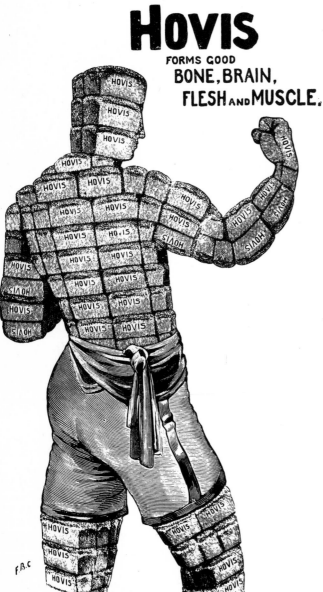

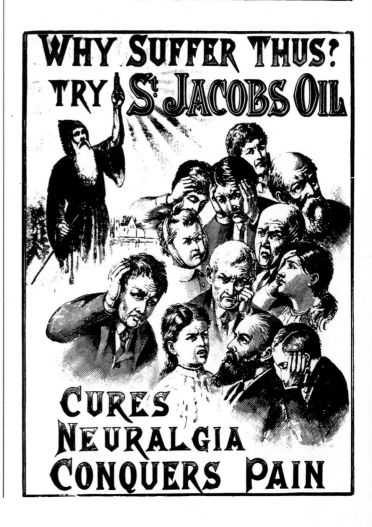

# "WHAT ARE THE WILD WAVES SAYING?"
# TRY BEECHAM'S PILLS.

## THE WORLD'S MEDICINE.

From the earliest days of medicinal science no antidote has achieved such a reputation as

## BEECHAM'S PILLS.

Their fame has reached the uttermost parts of the earth; their curative power is universally acknowledged to a degree unprecedented in the annals of physical research; and it is echoed from shore to shore that for Bilious and Nervous Disorders, Indigestion with its dreaded allies, and for assisting nature in her wondrous functions, they are

### WORTH A GUINEA A BOX.

# 'What do We Live for, if not to Make Life less difficult for Each Other?'—George Eliot.

We shut our eyes, the flowers bloom on; | We choose the shadow, but the sun
We murmur, but the corn-ears fill; | That casts it shines behind us still.

*And each good thought or action moves the dark world nearer to the sun.*—Whittier.

# LIGHT WHEN THOU ELSE WERT BLIND!
## SYMPATHY!
### STRENGTH WHEN LIFE'S SURGES RUDEST ROLL.

## Millais' Great Xmas Heart!

"Millais himself was occasionally induced to repeat the following anecdote, which is said by a personal friend to be new: I found myself (said the late P.R.A.) seated one evening at a rather grand dinner, next to a very pretty gushing girl, to whom I had not been introduced. She fired into conversation directly she had finished her soup, and as it was May began it with the inevitable question, 'I suppose you've been to the Academy?' I replied that I had. 'And did you notice the Millais'? Didn't you think they were awful daubs? I can't imagine how such things ever get hung——!' She was going on gaily in the same strain, while I sat silent, when suddenly the amused smiles of those around her and the significant hush brought her to a sudden *stop*. She coloured rather painfully, and whispered to me in a frightened voice, 'For heaven's sake, what have I done? Have I said anything dreadful? Do tell me.' 'Not now,' I replied, 'eat your dinner in peace, and I'll tell you by-and-by.' She did so, rather miserably, vainly trying to extract from me at intervals what the matter was, and when the dessert came I filled up her glass with champagne, and told her to gulp it down *very quickly* when I counted three. She obeyed without protest, and I took the opportunity when she *couldn't speak. I grasped her hand and said, 'I am Millais, let's be Friends.'*"

**MORAL:**—*Never blend Pain or Pride with the meanest thing that feels.*—Wordsworth

## AND SUCH IS HUMAN LIFE—SO GLIDING ON; IT GLIMMERS LIKE A METEOR, AND IS GONE.

## WHAT HIGHER AIM CAN MAN ATTAIN THAN CONQUEST OVER HUMAN PAIN?

IMPORTANT TO TRAVELLERS AT HOME AND ABROAD.—"Did the world stand still or did the generation that is to be benefit very fully by the experience gathered by their predecessors, but little necessity would exist for dwelling upon the special recommendations of ENO'S world-famous 'FRUIT SALT.' *It is not too much to say that its merits have been published, tested, and approved literally from pole to pole, and that its cosmopolitan popularity to-day presents one of the most signal illustrations of commercial enterprise to be found in our trading records.* In view of the constant and steady influx of new buyers into all the markets of the world, it is impossible to rest on laurels, however arduously won or freshly gathered; and for this reason I have pleasure in again, though briefly, directing the attention of readers of this journal to the genuine qualities possessed by ENO'S 'FRUIT SALT.' *Residents in the fever-haunted regions to be found in some of our colonial possessions, travellers at home and abroad, dwellers in the tropics, the bon vivant no less than the man to whom the recommendation, 'Eat and be merry,' is a sarcasm and a gibe—one and all may, with advantage to themselves, be reminded of a remedy that meets their special requirements with a success approaching the miraculous."—European Mail.*

**STIMULANTS.—CONGESTION OF THE LIVER.**—Experience shows that Acidulated Sherbet masked with Sugar, Hazardous Brain Tipples, or any form of Pick-me-up, Porter, Mild Ales, Port Wine, Dark Sherries, Sweet Champagne, Liqueurs, and Brandies, are all very apt to disagree, while Light White Wines, and Gin or Old Whisky, largely diluted with pure Mineral Water, will be found the least objectionable. ENO'S 'FRUIT SALT' is PARTICULARLY ADAPTED for ANY constitutional WEAKNESS of the LIVER. It possesses the power of preparation where digestion has been disturbed or lost, and PLACES the INVALID on the RIGHT TRACK to HEALTH.

ONLY TRUTH CAN GIVE TRUE REPUTATION—ONLY REALITY CAN BE OF REAL PROFIT—THE SECRET OF SUCCESS—STERLING HONESTY OF PURPOSE—WITHOUT IT LIFE IS A SHAM.

*The value of ENO'S 'FRUIT SALT' cannot be told. Its success in Europe, Asia, Africa, America, Australia, and New Zealand proves it.*

THERE IS NO DOUBT THAT where it has been taken in the earliest stages of a disease it has, in innumerable instances, PREVENTED what would otherwise have been a SERIOUS ILLNESS. The effect of ENO'S 'FRUIT SALT' upon any DISORDERED, SLEEPLESS, and FEVERISH condition is SIMPLY MARVELLOUS. It is, in fact, NATURE'S OWN REMEDY, and an UNSURPASSED ONE.

CAUTION.—*Examine each Bottle, and see the Capsule is marked ENO'S 'FRUIT SALT.' Without it you have been imposed upon by WORTHLESS imitations.*

## Prepared only by J. C. ENO, Ltd., 'FRUIT SALT' WORKS, LONDON, S.E., by J. C. ENO'S PATENT.

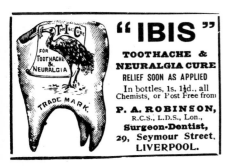

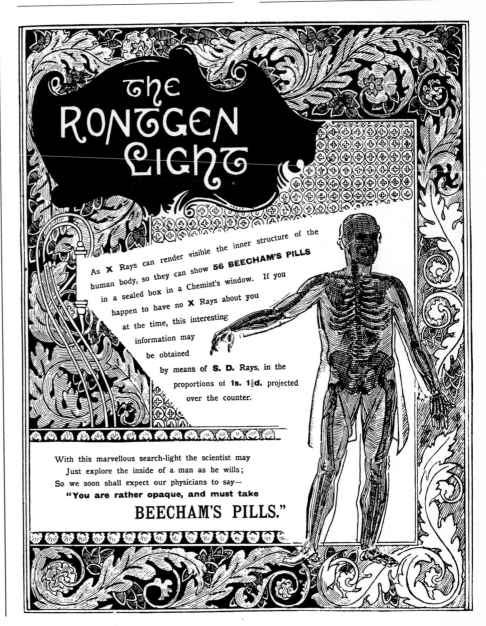

# BEAUTY

Part of the function of advertisers has always been to sell dreams, and the dream they induce with the greatest success is the dream of beauty. Their incantations are directed chiefly to women, for there are few women who do not desire to be beautiful and attractive to men. Unfortunately men do not always desire the same things in women. In one age they wish them to be petite and provocative, as in the age of Louis XV; in another their ideal is tall and stately, proud and a little austere. At one period the 'fine woman' is admired; at another the slim girl, not sexless indeed, but certainly androgyne. Women know this and model themselves accordingly, with a decree of plasticity which never ceases to astonish the social historian.

In the period covered by the illustrations in the present volume there was little doubt of the accepted ideal. The eighteenth century *petite femme* and the mid-nineteenth century 'little woman' were alike 'out'. In their place was

> A daughter of the gods, divinely tall,
> And most divinely fair.

A woman such as Burne-Jones or Lord Leighton would have liked to paint. And lo! suddenly, the world was full of such women with small heads, straight backs, long legs—and a rather tight waist.

We can see this quite plainly in the corset advertisements; and we can note something else: the daring of the corset manufacturers in the last quarter of the nineteenth century. In former ages it was only in erotic prints that the costume historian could study feminine underwear. Now he was admitted to the bedroom even in the chaste pages of *The Illustrated London News*. He could watch the development of foundation garments from the primitive all-round pressure of the '70's and '80's to the 'health corset' of the closing years of the century. This threw the hips back and the bust forward and produced the curious swan-like stance of the woman of the period, a stance which has been humorously described as that of a lady at a garden party 'about to shake hands with the lower classes'. It satisfied the ideal

of the time but, of course, from the health point of view it was just as deleterious as the models that preceded it.

Apart from corsets, the underclothes depicted, however they may have excited the imagination of the late Victorians, seem curiously unattractive. Those long, clumsy ankle-length bloomers, those knitted combinations: were they really the wear of fashionable women? The answer is undoubtedly yes. The footwear too, might be expected to appeal to the shoe-fetishist, but surely to no-one else.

Given the hair-dressing fashion of the period false hair was essential to all but the most fortunate. We find advertisements of 'Curled Fringes', of 'Half, Three-quarter, or Full Wigs', of 'Natural Waved Bandeaux' and other 'Aids to Nature'. And, of course, the purveyors of hair dye do not suggest for a moment that you wanted to dye your hair: you merely wanted to 'restore' it to its natural colour. Gentlemen dyed their whiskers and you could buy a preparation to enable you to 'train your moustache the way it should go'.

'A Healthy, Soft and Beautiful Skin' could be obtained by using The New Patent Parisian Vaporiser or Beetham's Glycerine and Cucumber Lotion. Cosmetics are very discreetly handled. Lip-sticks, even disguised as lip-salves, were still in the future; but we find advertisements of eye-pencils promising the 'Power of Fascination' to the eye. When dealing with make-up the advertisers thought it more discreet to speak French. 'Love Powder' would have been altogether too coarse a phrase: '*Poudre d'Amour*' sounded much better. *Plus ça change. . . .*

One cannot help wondering to whom such advertisements were directed. Presumably to the upper classes, or to those daughters of the successful merchants who hoped, one day, to be accepted by the County. Today, advertisers cast a much wider net, and there is scarcely a girl of any age or class who does not hope to make herself more attractive to her predestined mate by purchasing somebody's beauty preparation. The democratization of beauty! Why not?

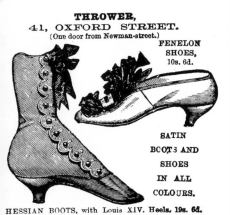

41

"Value for Money."

"The secret of success."

# THE INTERNATIONAL FUR STORE,

## 163, REGENT STREET, 163.  T. S. JAY, Manager.

44

45

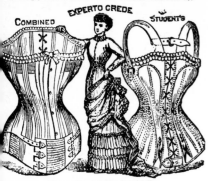

47

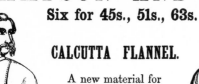

49

51

53

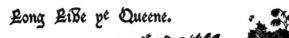

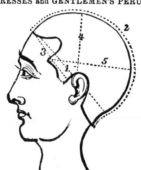

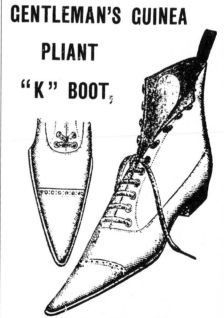

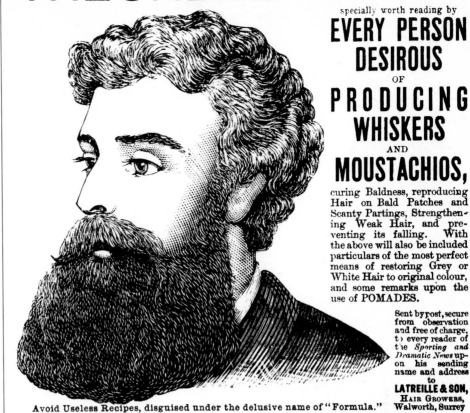

57

**THE WEDDING MORNING.**

What happy recollections the above Picture recalls to those who have helped a Bride with her toilet! Friends ask themselves, Has the Bride a thorough knowledge of all the duties of a household, especially of that ever-recurring worry, Washing Day and Spring Cleaning? Does she know what

# SUNLIGHT SOAP

can do? Does she know that for a few pence, without boiling or bleaching, she can, by using SUNLIGHT SOAP, have all the household linen washed at home and made to look white as snow and fresh as roses?

Happy is the bride who has been instructed in these matters, because it is on such simple household details as these that the future happiness and comfort of herself and husband must depend!

58

59

# THE LOUIS VELVETEEN.

## NOTE WELL!

The word "LOUIS" in connection with this Velveteen is spelled

## "L·O·U·I·S,"

### AND IN NO OTHER WAY.

"LE FOLLET" says:

The "LOUIS" VELVETEEN, though draping with the rich folds of Genoa velvet—which its subtle shadows and beautiful "bloom" cause it exactly to resemble—is infinitely lighter in wear. It possesses, also, an incalculable advantage, which even alone would account for the favour it receives from those who understand the ART OF DRESS, viz., by a particular method of locking the pile, this resists any injury from creasing, dust, or even rain, and preserves the freshness of its appearance to the last day of its wear.

## THE "LOUIS" VELVETEEN IS SOLD BY ALL DRAPERS THROUGHOUT THE KINGDOM.

EVERY YARD of the genuine bears the name of "LOUIS," and the wear of every yard, from the cheapest quality to the best, GUARANTEED.

## HILDER AND GODBOLD

ARE now making a grand display of PARISIAN MILLINERY at their extensive Show Rooms, 10, 11, and 12, Leicester-street, Leicester-square, W. The styles are of the best, while the prices are at least one-third less than usually charged. Ladies should send for our New Illustrated Fashion Book and Catalogue, 32 Pages, post free, 3d.

### SUBJOINED ARE ILLUSTRATIONS OF CHILDREN'S HATS.

"LOUISE."
Straw lined full Satin Merveilleux, Lace and Bows of Shaded Ribbons, 12s. 9d.

"LILLIE."
In Straw, trimmed Shaded Ribbon, Bow and Silk Aigrette, 12s. 9d. and 14s. 9d.

"CHERRY RIPE."
Cream or White Spanish Lace, lined with Pale Blue, or any colour, Bows of same, 19s. 6d.

"MAUD."
Straw, trimmed Lace and Ribbon Rosettes, lined full Lace, 14s. 9d.

ANY OF THE ABOVE PACKED IN STRONG BOX AND SENT CARRIAGE FREE TO ANY PART OF THE KINGDOM 2s. 6D. EXTRA.

HILDER & GODBOLD, FRENCH MILLINERS, 10, 11, & 12, LEICESTER ST., LEICESTER SQ., W

61

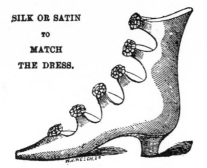

65

THE SPECIALITÉ CORSET

leads the way all the world over to Woman's greatest ambition — A GOOD FIGURE

Regd. No. 25,540.

TYPE 1.—Long waist, in Black Italian Cloth and Real Whalebone, 19/6 complete; in Black Satin, 27/6.
TYPE 1.—Extra long waist, in Black Italian Cloth and Real Whalebone, 21/- complete; in Black Satin, 29/6, complete.
TYPE 1.—Long waist, cut longer below the waist, and extra fully boned to give greater support to stout figures, 25/-.
TYPE 2.—Long waist, in White Coutille and Real Whalebone, 18/6 complete.

TYPE 2.—Extra long waist, in White Coutille and Real Whalebone, 21/- complete.
TYPE 2.—In Pink or White Silk Coutille, cool and comfortable, without lining, cut low for evening wear, 33/- complete.
TYPE 3.—Medium long waist, in White Coutille, with Real Whalebone, 16/6 complete; in Black Italian Cloth and Real Whalebone, 18 6 complete.
THE "SPÉCIALITÉ" SPORTS CORSET for Cycling, Riding, Rowing. Golfing, or Tennis, White Coutille, and fitted with best Real Whalebone. 16/6 complete.

CAUTION.—See that every pair is stamped inside "Dickins & Jones," without which none are genuine.

Sole Agents for the "Spécialité Corsets"—New South Wales, DAVID JONES & CO., Sydney: Madras, Bangalore, and Kola, "THE ENGLISH WAREHOUSE"; Calcutta, WHITEAWAY, LAIDLAW

# DICKINS & JONES, REGENT ST., LONDON.

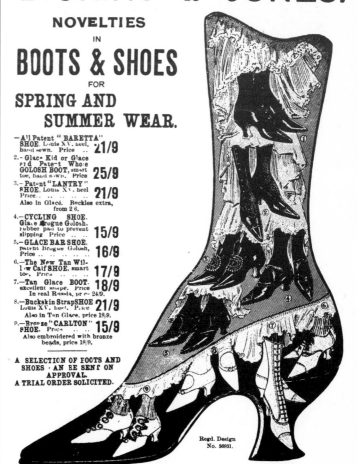
67

## THE "NOVITY" COMBINATIONS.

# PETER ROBINSON

Ltd.,

## OXFORD - ST.

# LORD BYRON'S
## HEROINE.

"Nothing earthly could surpass her,
Save thine incomparable oil, Macassar."
("Don Juan." Canto I.)

A splendid testimony this of the poet's high appreciation of the merits of

## ROWLANDS' MACASSAR OIL.

His Lordship preserved his fine head of hair by the use of this Oil, and recommended it to all his acquaintances as being the best and safest preserver and beautifier of the hair. Also in a golden colour for fair hair. Bottles, **3s. 6d., 7s., 10s. 6d.** (equal to 4 small).

UNDER THE DISTINGUISHED PATRONAGE OF H.R.H. PRINCESS OF WALES and H.R.H. DUCHESS OF YORK.

THE DUCHESS OF YORK says: "She thinks the Flower Shield a most ingenious invention, and wishes it success." The custom of wearing sprays of flowers at Balls, Receptions, and Assemblies of the *élite* is a growing one, and, following the Royal example, the coming season is likely to see a considerable extension of the fashion. Ladies hitherto have been extremely inconvenienced in having to adjust their sprays *after* arrival (frequently in a crowded cloak-room), or else run the risk of the flowers being disarranged and crushed by the opera cloak. The "Princess" Flower Shield is a perfect protection, is removed in an instant upon entering the ball room, and fits inside pocket of opera cloak when not in use.

**PRINCESS PATENT FLOWER SHIELD.**

It is compact, light, and easily adjusted, and when worn does not disturb the dress in any way, or interfere with the fall of the cloak. "A" Quality, Superior Nickel Plated, No. 1, 2/6; No. 2, 5/-; No. 3, 7/6. "B" Quality, Silver Plated, No. 1, 1/6; No. 2, 2/6; No. 3, 3/6. Of all Drapers, Florists, and Costumiers in the United Kingdom. If you cannot obtain in your neighbourhood, send stamps or Postal Order direct to the—

**PATENT FLOWER SHIELD CO.,**
42, BASINGHALL STREET, LONDON, E.C.

NO, DEAR, IT WOULD BE IMPOSSIBLE TO CRUSH THEM.

## SCHOOL BOX, WITH OUTFIT COMPLETE,
### For Boy of 11 Years, £8 1s. 10d.
### (SEE ILLUSTRATED CATALOGUE.)

## SCHOOL OUTFITS.

Messrs. SAMUEL BROTHERS, Ltd., are prepared to supply COMPLETE OUTFITS in accordance with the regulations specially prescribed by the leading

## PUBLIC SCHOOLS & COLLEGES
### INCLUDING

| | | |
|---|---|---|
| ETON | HARROW | RUGBY |
| MARLBOROUGH | WINCHESTER | CLIFTON |
| HAILEYBURY | WELLINGTON | WESTMINSTER |
| ST. PAUL'S | CHARTERHOUSE | DULWICH |
| CHELTENHAM | SHREWSBURY | SHERBORNE |

*List of Outfit for any of the above Public Schools forwarded Post Free on Application.*

WILLIAM KEEL'S DELIVERY VAN.

W. KEEL'S HAT MANUFACTORY DUDLEY ST. BIRMINGHAM

IN EVERY SHAPE,

FROM 5/6 TO 16/-

LINFOOT, MORRIS, & Co. EASY ROW, BIRM.

DUDLEY STREET, ONLY.

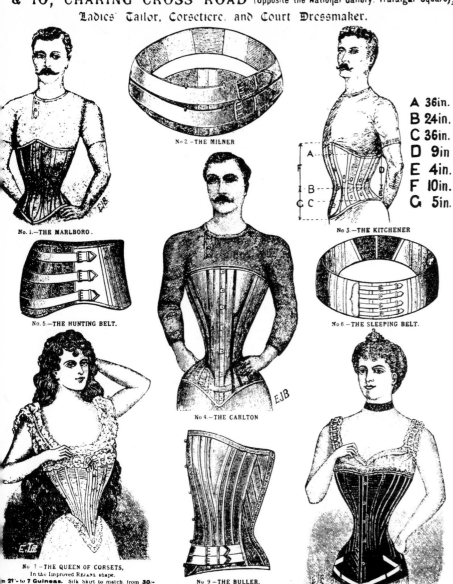

69

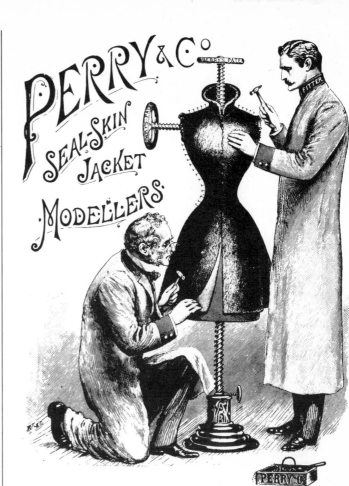

71

Perhaps it is from the miscellaneous advertisements that one can learn most about life in late Victorian England: all the things that formal histories leave out. It was above all an age of invention, all kinds of gadgets were coming on to the market, some doomed to failure by their very absurdity, some destined to develop into the accepted appliances of today. We find a primitive form of washing machine; a Reservoir Pen, the ancestor of all fountain pens; a 'Safety' wringer and mangle, an early phonograph. We can watch the development of the bicycle from the alarming 'penny-farthing' to models indistinguishable from those still in use. We see its rival, the tricycle, one example worked by a liveried footman pedalling manfully behind. We are offered a typewriter for three guineas and informed that 'the entire correspondence of a business house can be done with it'.

Among the absurdities are a patent automatic mustard pot, a window cleaner worked by a string (if it ever worked at all) and a Work-Fastener which screwed on to the edge of the dining room table and held whatever the lady was sewing in a firm grip. At Thornhill's in New Bond Street you could buy the most surprising objects: a silver fish which was at once a pencil, a two-bladed knife and a whistle for calling cabs; a Smoking Lamp (i.e. one which provided a constant small flame for lighting cigars) shaped like a serpent; a pipe-rack in the form of a miniature step-ladder and dangerous looking Tricycle Skates ('For use at Home or Abroad') each skate consisting of two large wheels and one small one.

There is a surprising number of advertisements for Ladder Tapes which could be used, according to one head-line, as 'A Modern Method of Elopement'—hardly an inducement, one would have thought, for *pater familias* to buy them. Actually they formed part of the inevitable venetian blinds.

The Victorian household lived in constant dread of fires (Ladder Tapes might have come in useful here) and the firm of Merryweather, in Long Acre, special-ized in such devices as the Chute Fire Escape, 'as supplied to Queen Anne's Mansions', and an even more ingenious Kit-Bag Fire Escape, 'as supplied to H.M. the Khedive of Egypt'. Empire builders could buy an even more surprising invention: a 'small case' into which could be packed enough folding furniture to equip a bed-room—'invaluable to Colonists, Officers' Quarters, Shooting Boxes' etc.

From some of the advertisements we obtain fascinating glimpses of domestic staff at their various employments. We see a trim maid (in a bustle) bending over a kitchen range of alarming complexity, and another, in a surprisingly short skirt and décolleté bodice, making 'Bright Reflections' in the dish covers by means of Monkey Brand Soap. Cook, kitchen-maid and page boy are blown off their feet in the kitchen by an 'Explosion due to Incrustations caused by Hard Water, preventable by "Anti-Calcaire"' water softener. An advertisement of a Kitchen Furnishing List shows everything that servants could require from gridirons to dustpans—and all for £11. 3. 10d. A dramatic scene of a fight between two maids points the moral that although Davy's Diamond Cement 'will not mend broken heads', it will mend almost everything else from china and papier maché to cigar-holders and picture frames. It could also be used 'for fastening tips on billiard cues'.

When we ascend to the living quarters of the Victorian house we can study, in admirable detail, the furnishing of a bedroom in the 1890's: brass bedstead with a canopy over it, tiled washhandstand with jug and ewer (the other porcelain 'article' concealed by a curtain) and a very handsome *armoire à glace*. In the middle stands the lady in her corset, presumably waiting for her maid to release her from its steel or whalebone grip. What we see reflected in all these advertisements is the domestic life of the prosperous Middle Classes who were, after all, the main readers of the magazines in which they appeared.

## MOURNING ORDERS IN THE COUNTRY.

Messrs JAY'S experienced Assistants and Dress-fitters travel to any part of the kingdom, free of expense to purchasers. They take with them Dresses, Mantles, and Millinery, besides Patterns of Materials, all marked in Plain Figures, and at the same price as if purchased at the warehouse. Reasonable estimates are also given for Household Mourning.

# JAY'S, REGENT STREET, LONDON.

74

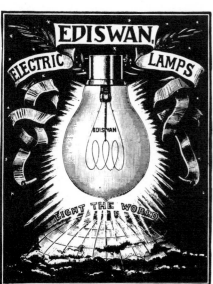

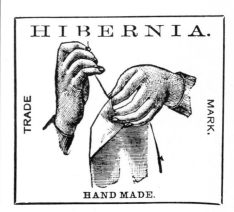
75

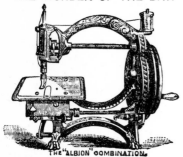

# PUT OUT THE FIRE BEFORE IT GETS A GOOD HOLD,
## AND THUS SAVE LIFE AND PROPERTY.

**BALL-ROOM PERILS.** A YOUNG LADY'S LIFE SAVED by the prompt use of a HARDEN "STAR" HAND GRENADE. The many terrible calamities that have marked the present Season should emphasise the importance of having these sure and effective Fire Extinguishers ready for every emergency. They should be on every Staircase. In every Private Residence—In every Institution. In every Public Building. In every Ship. The HARDEN "STAR" HAND GRENADES are the original and only practicable and reliable FIRE EXTINGUISHING GRENADE KNOWN. Always ready; will not freeze; cannot get out of order; can be used efficiently by man, woman, or child. AVOID THE IMITATIONS, WHICH ARE NONE OF THEM HERMETICALLY SEALED, and are CONSEQUENTLY WORTHLESS. The Blue Melon-shaped Grenade, with a "Star" blown in the Bottle, alone is genuine, and its colour and form are registered. 48s. per dozen net ; of all respectable ironmongers. **THE HARDEN "STAR" HAND GRENADE FIRE EXTINGUISHER** COMPANY, Limited, No. 1, Holborn Viaduct, London ; 54, Victoria-street, Liverpool; 124, Queen-street, Glasgow; 18, Rue Caumartin, Paris. LATEST AWARD "**THE GOLD MEDAL**" OF THE ARCHITECTURAL AND BUILDING TRADES EXHIBITION, LONDON, 1886.

The HARDEN "STAR" HAND GRENADE FIRE EXTINGUISHER has been the means of saving the following Premises and Warehouses from Destruction by Fire, for which we hold Testimonials in each case :—

Derbyshire lace factory saved by means of the Harden "Star." Messrs. Tatham Bros., Ilkeston, March 3, 1885.

Fire caused by methylated spirit extinguished by means of the Harden "Star."—Messrs. Walker and Son, 35, High-street, Maidenhead, March 2, 1885.

Joiners' shop saved by means of the Harden "Star." Messrs. Penny and Co., Lincoln, April 4, 1885.

Dining-rooms saved by means of the Harden "Star."—Mr. R. W. Blackbourn, 8, Blanket-row, Hull, Aug. 30, 1885.

Birkdale Farm Reformatory School saved by means of the Harden "Star." Gov. Shee, Ainsdale, near Southport, July 1, 1885.

Lithographic establishment saved by means of the Harden "Star."— W. Brownlee, Glasgow, July 27, 1885.

Life and property saved at the West-End.— At the residence of the Rev. H. P. Gurney, M.A., 2, Powis-square, Feb. 11, 1886, by means of the Harden "Star."

The Villiers Hotel, Douglas, Isle of Man, saved by means of the Harden "Star."—Aug. 14, 1885.

Marver and Collingham's premises, Lincoln, saved by means of the Harden "Star."—Aug. 19, 1885.

Large bootmaking establishment saved by means of the Harden "Star." — A. and W. Flatau, Ropemaker-street, Finsbury, E.C., Dec. 24, 1884.

Valuable oil mills saved by means of the Harden "Star." Messrs. Foster Brothers, Gloucester, Feb. 24, 1885.

Dye-works saved by means of the Harden "Star." Wm. Bishop, Stroudwater, Jan. 6, 1885.

Elastic web manufactory saved by means of the Harden "Star." Messrs. Dalby Bros. and Co., Leicester, March 25, 1885.

Premises and valuable stock saved by means of the Harden "Star." Mr. G. Heaven, 6 and 7, Edgbaston-street, Birmingham, Jan. 20, 1886.

Life saved owing to the Harden "Star." Mrs. Gibson, St. John's, Worcester, Feb. 19, 1886.

Messrs. C. Ward and Son's premises, 2, West Chapel-street, Mayfair, W., saved by means of the Harden "Star." April 27, 1886.

The Harden "Star" was the means of saving Mr. J. T. Whitesmith's premises and stock, Mill-street, Kidderminster.

Country residence saved by means of the Harden "Star."—C. W. Wilson, Rigmaden Park, Kirkby Lonsdale, March 29, 1885.

Large business premises in Paris saved by means of the Harden "Star."— Messrs. Esnault, Pelterie, Ainé et Cie, 5, Rue St. Fiacre, Feb. 1, 1886.

Stand saved at the "INVENTIONS" EXHIBITION owing to the Harden Star. City Rubber Stamp Co., 10, Ludgate-hill, Sept. 16, 1885.

QUEEN CHARLOTTE'S LYING-IN HOSPITAL, Marylebone-road, three outbreaks of the fire suppressed by the Harden "Star," May 4, 1885.

House and hop-kilns saved by means of the Harden "Star."- G. V. Knight, Hale, Farnham, March 22, 1886.

And many others.

**Special Notice.—** In the HARDEN "STAR" HAND GRENADE FIRE EXTINGUISHER the whole of the Extinguishing Liquid is expended in the Fire itself, there being no loss in delivering it from the Hand, an important and distinctive advantage over other so-called Hand Fire Extinguishers.

# TITAN PATENT SOAP

**WILL WASH CLOTHES.**

HUDSON'S SOAP *is a pure DRY Soap in fine powder, and dissolves immediately in hot or cold water. Sold Everywhere, in 1lb., ½lb., and ¼lb. packets. For family use, in parcels containing 6 or 12 packets; also in 14lb. and 28lb. boxes. Invaluable for Washing Flannels and Winter Underclothing, as well as Linen Shirts, Collars, Sheets, Table Cloths, &c. Try a penny packet.*

A PURE SOAP in fine powder.

# HUDSON'S
## SOAP

LEAVES NO SMELL.

A BRIGHT LIGHT ON A DARK NIGHT!—*Nothing cleans the chimneys and globes of lamps so well as HUDSON'S SOAP dissolved in warm water. This is only one of the many uses to which Hudson's Soap can be applied. It should be used daily for washing clothes, linen, plates, dishes, knives, forks, and everything.*

79

80

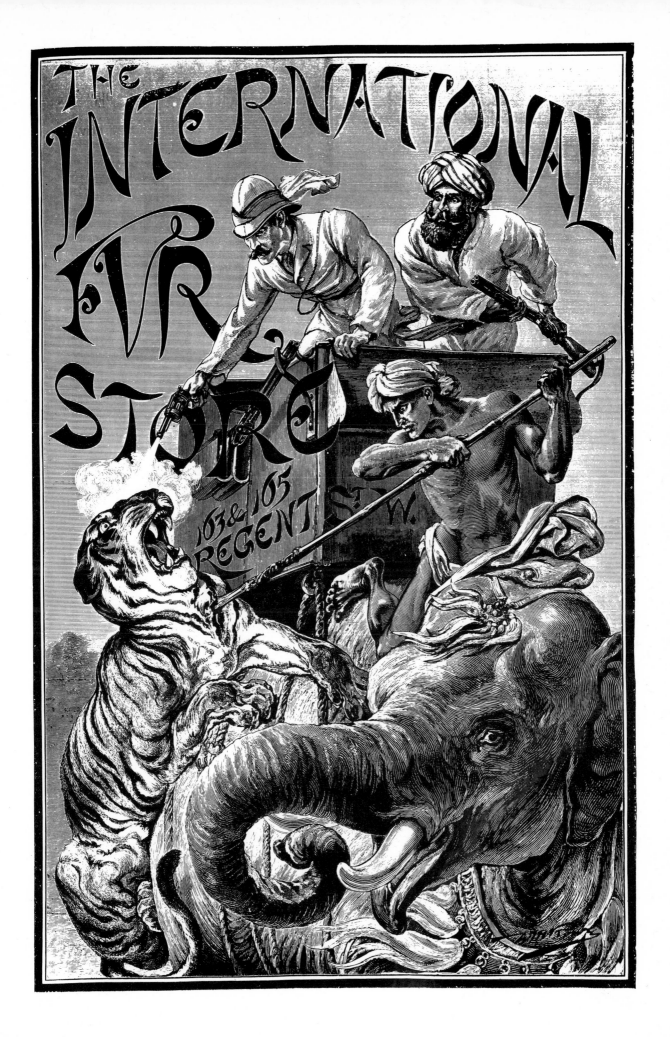

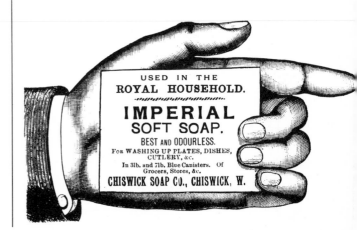

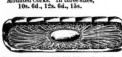

84

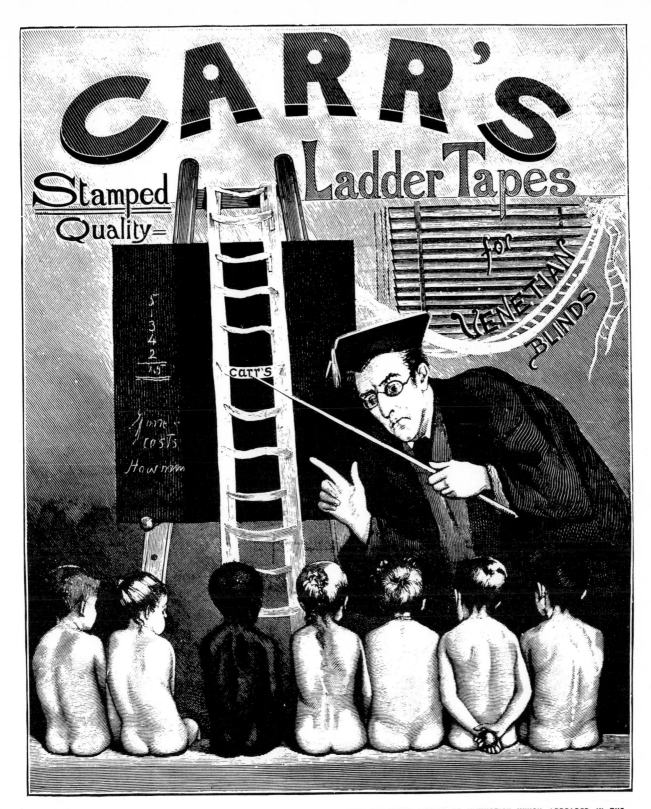

# CARR'S

## Stamped Quality=

## Ladder Tapes

### for VENETIAN BLINDS

carr's

# A ROD IN

# PICKLE

For those who sell, under the name of "CARR'S TAPES," any but the best and stamped quality.

85

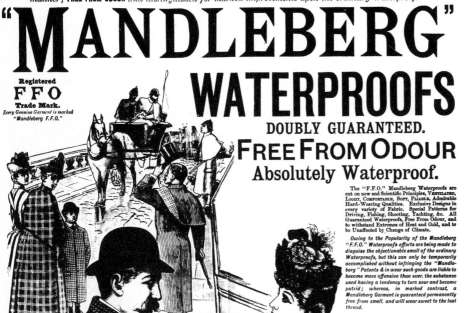

89

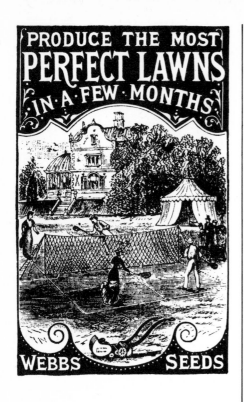

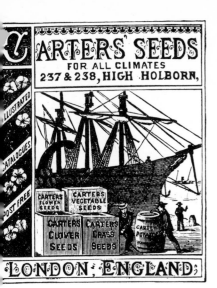

91

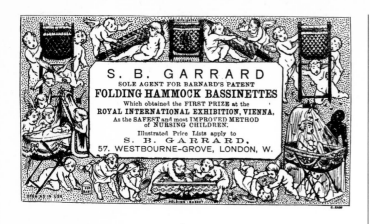

For Pots and Pans.    For Mantels and Marble.    For Fire-irons and Gas Globes.    For a thousand things in the Household, the Factory,
the Shop, and on Shipboard.

## WILL DO A DAY'S WORK IN AN HOUR.

Sold by Grocers, Ironmongers, and Chemists everywhere.   If not obtainable near you, send **4**ᴰ· in stamps for full-size Bar, free by post,
or **1**ˢ· for Three Bars, free by post (mentioning the "Illustrated London News"), to

# B. BROOKE & CO., 36 to 40, York Road, King's Cross, London.

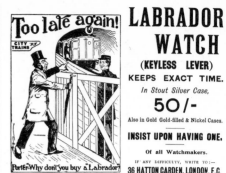

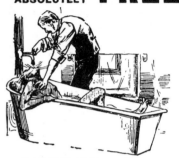
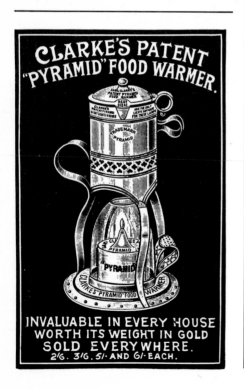

94

95

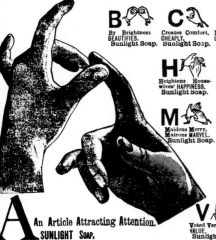

MAKE ROOM FOR MONKEY BRAND!

WON'T WASH CLOTHES.                    WON'T WASH CLOTHES.
BROOKE'S

# MONKEY BRAND
SOAP

## FOR KITCHEN TABLES AND FLOORS, LINOLEUM AND OILCLOTHS.

*For Polishing Metals, Marble, Paint, Cutlery, Crockery, Machinery, Baths, Stair-Rods.*

FOR STEEL, IRON, BRASS AND COPPER VESSELS, FIRE-IRONS, MANTELS, &c.          REMOVES RUST, DIRT, STAINS, TARNISH, &c.

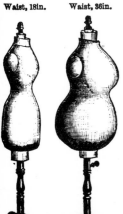

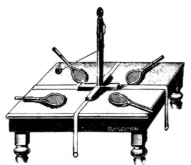

99

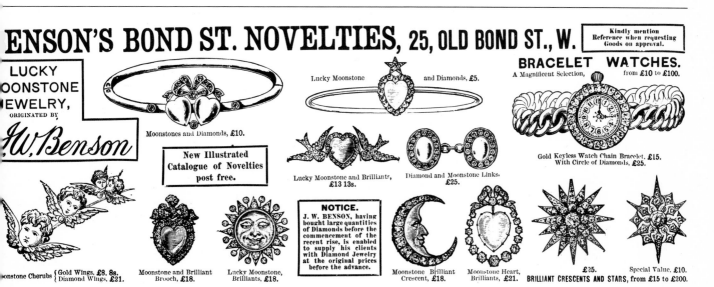

HUDSON'S SOAP is a pure Dry Soap in fine Powder, in 1lb., ½lb., and ¼lb. packets—softens all waters, makes a foaming lather, and keeps the clothes a good colour.
HUDSON'S SOAP is excellent for washing Flannels and Woollen Underclothing, as well as Linen, Shirts, Collars, Sheets, Table Cloths, &c.
HUDSON'S SOAP for Washing-up. Hudson's is as good for Plates, Dishes, Knives, Forks, &c., as for Washing Clothes. Hudson's leaves no Smell.

# PLEASURE

Much can be learned of a civilization by the study of its favourite amusements and pastimes, and the late Victorian Age is no exception. Up to the middle of the century riding and hunting had been almost the only outdoor pursuits. Then came, in succession, archery, croquet and lawn tennis, originally called Sphaïristike. There was also, by the middle of the '90's, Lawn and House Golf, the 'latest popular game now in use at Balmoral, Marlborough House, Sandringham and White Lodge'. Marine Golf could be played on the decks of yachts 'with sliders instead of balls', as 'used by the Prince of Wales, Emperor of Germany etc.' All these required special apparatus, and sports outfitting rapidly became a prosperous business, while the popularity of river sports induced a boom in house-boats, punts and Canadian canoes.

Then there was the seaside to which every Middle Class family now made its annual pilgrimage; and we find a whole series of advertisements for bathing costumes, covering the female body from neck to calf and dignified by the names of *French* seaside resorts: Biarritz, Mentone, Boulogne and Trouville. It must have been very gratifying to young ladies to wear a Biarritz costume, even if their parents were merely taking them to Eastbourne.

We have already glanced at the growing popularity of the bicycle and the tricycle and noted its evolution from the clumsy contraptions of the '70's to the neat models of twenty years later. Cycling was, of course, still a 'sport', and the really smart thing to do was to send your groom with the machine to Battersea Park on Sunday morning. You then drove there in your carriage, mounted your bicycle, rode several times round the Park, handed the machine over to your groom and drove home for luncheon.

Indoor pastimes began to multiply, no doubt in answer to what must often have been the excruciating boredom of an evening passed in the family circle. Advertisers advised parents to 'keep the Boys at Home' by installing a billiard table. It need not be full size and a miniature version ('Dull Evenings Made Merry') could be purchased for as little as £7. Then there was ping-pong and blow football, and if you were musical you could buy an early form of the phonograph (one advertisement already calls it a gramophone) or even install a piano. And there was a Patented Music Turner—a most misguided invention, one would have thought, since turning the leaves for a lady was one of the recognised modes of polite flirtation.

If everything else failed you could 'Learn to Hypnotize' or do conjuring tricks, the complete apparatus for the latter costing no more than a guinea. Or you could teach your bird 'to sing and whistle popular airs' by means of a Bird Organ, a kind of musical box worked with a crank. You might even read a book with the aid of Watt's Patent Book and Newspaper Holder which rested on your stomach and was kept in place by a string round the neck.

If you were a gentleman you could smoke a cigar while reclining in the Sir Walter Raleigh Smoking Chair, or the Folding Yankee Hammock Chair, the 'practical utility' of which 'has not been equalled in the Cabinet or Upholsterer's craft' and 'folds into the compass of a Butler's Tray'. Or, of course, you could eat and drink, although few of the advertisements suggest any of the higher reaches of gastronomy. Tea was much advertised, and also cocoa of which the late Victorians appear to have consumed inordinate amounts. It seems to have been considered a suitable beverage even on a house-boat at Henley. We need not envy them such delights. What we might indeed envy is the fact that a *barrel* of oysters could be obtained from The Cowes Parcels Post Native Oyster Supply Association—for ten shillings.

Indeed what strikes the modern reader most forcibly is the extreme cheapness of everything. One must, of course, make allowance for the fall in the value of money, but, all the same, some of the prices quoted make it plain that it was easier for (shall we say) the city clerk to have a night out with his girl friend than it would be for his equivalent today.

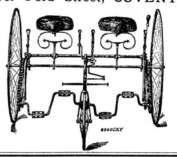

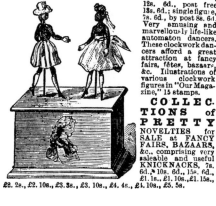

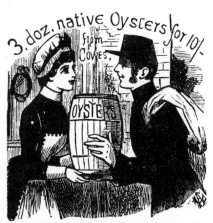

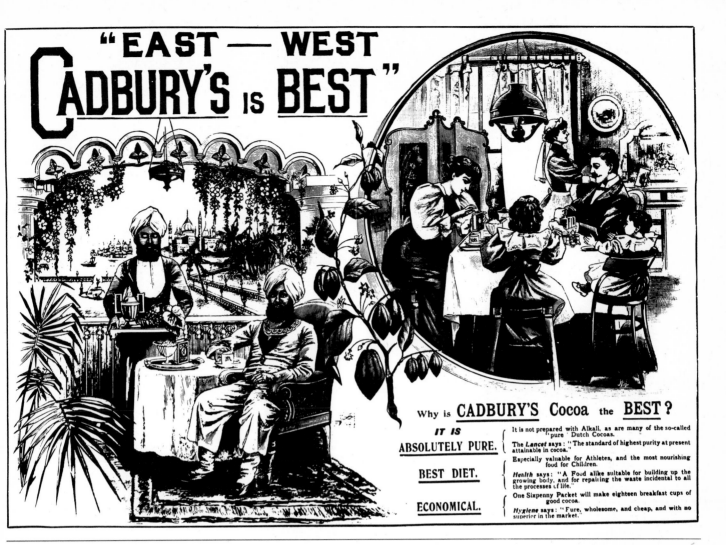

III

# Chas. Morrell's Christmas Toys & Games.

**"THE CIVET CAT,"** 368, OXFORD ST., LONDON, W.

THE LARGEST & CHOICEST STOCK IN LONDON.

**ALL ORDERS TO BE PREPAID.**

Boxes containing CHRISTMAS TREE ORNAMENTS, Beads, Candles, Clips, Fancy Boxes, Flags, &c, for trimming Trees, at 5/-, 7/6, 10/6, 15/6, to £10.

**MORRELL'S CHRISTMAS-TREE ORNAMENTS, &c.** Small Toys, Dolls, and Fancy Articles for Christmas Trees in enormous variety. Trees trimmed to order to any amount. Artificial Trees made to order in any size, fitted with or without the Electric Light.

**DOLLS' HOUSES** in great variety, with 2, 3, or 4 Rooms, from 3/6 to £10. 10s.

**LARGE OAK STABLE,** as per illustration, containing Skin covered Horses, Horse Clothing, Harness to take off, Loose Box, Carriage, Stable Fittings, price £7; smaller size, £4. Also a large variety of good Stables, from 5/6 to £3.

**CLOCKWORK BEETLE.** When wound up, crawls along the floor, and flaps its wings. Price, 1/- by post 3d. extra.

**METAL SOLDIERS.**—Royal Horse Artillery (London made), complete with quick-firing gun, levelling screw, and ammunition; splendid model. Price, 5/6; by post 6d. extra. Also Infantry and Cavalry Regiments in great variety, from 10½d. per box. A large selection of good Boxes of Metal Soldiers, all the latest novelties, Camps, Artillery, Pontoons, Reviews, Bands, Cycling Corps, Ballooning, Camel Corps, General Staff, &c., up to £3 per box.

**CATALOGUE POST FREE.**

Rocking and Tricycle Horses in all sizes.

*PARFUMERIE RÉGENCE*

**Catalogue Post Free.**

**SOLDIER DOLLS,** dressed as Grenadier, Hussar, Naval Officer, Black Watch, & several other patterns at 10/6 each.

**JOINTED DOLL,** dressed in velvet, trimmed fur, hand made clothes, to undress. Prices, 18/6, 21/-, 25/-, 28/-, 32/6, to 63/-.

**MODEL SHOPS** in great variety; Perfumer s, as per illustration, 21/-, 30/-, 40/-. Confectioner's (latest novelty), 35/-, 50/-. Grocer's, Poulterer's, Butcher's, Fruit Stalls, &c., from 5/6 to 60/-.

**THE MARVELLOUS AUTOMATIC CHAMPION PRIZE FIGHTERS.** Latest English Novelty. The figures are worked by the pressure of a r through an india-rubber tube attached to each. The arms and legs being composed of india-rubber the movements are rendered supple and natural. Can be worked by one or two persons, causing much fun and excitement. Post free, 10/6.

**All Orders to be Prepaid.**

**Latest novelty CLOCKWORK DOG,** jumps along playing battledore and shuttlecock. Price, 10/6.

New Mulatto JOINTED DOLLS 3/9, 4/9, 5/6, 6/6, to 16/6. Also common quality at 1/-, 1/6, 2/-, 2/6.

**NEW MODELS IN CARDBOARD FOR FITTING TOGETHER. THE SWITCHBACK,** with a small car that will run down the slopes, and a small lift to raise it again to the top. Length, when constructed, 27in.; height, 16in. Price, 1/-; by post 4½d. extra. Also the PYRAMIDICAL RAILWAY, GREAT WHEEL TOWER BRIDGE, &c.

**PRETTY JOINTED DOLL in Trunk,** with complete Trousseau, as illustrated. Price 63/-; smaller sizes at 50/-, 42/-, 35/-, 25/-, 21/-, 18/6, 15/6, 12/6, 10/6.

**NEW CLOCKWORK TRICYCLE,** with Cat rider, prettily d essed, price 10/6. Also larger size, with Cat, Dog, or Rabbit rider, elegantly dressed in Satin, raising hat while rid ng. Price, 21/-, 30/-.

**BABY TOYS** in great variety. Wool Sheep, Goats, Pigs, Lions, Donkeys, soft wool & fur toys, Rattles &c.

**WORKING MODEL HOT AIR ENGINE,** latest novelty. Will continue working as long as the lamp is burning; simple in working, no danger, as no water or steam is used. Prices, 5/6, 7/6, 10/6, 21/-, 28/-. Also working model Gas Engines, from 18/6.

**CLOCKWORK BICYCLE,** with rubber tyres, dog attached to side, 1/-.

**MECHANICAL CROCODILE,** when wound up crawls along floor, opening and shutting its mouth. Price, 1/-; by post 3d. extra.

**NEW SOFT WOOL RATTLE** for Babies Price 1/-; by post 3d. extra.

112

# UNITED MOTOR INDUSTRIES

## PARIS: 3 RUE MEYERBEER : PARIS.

*Telegraphic Address: "MAGNETO, PARIS."*                    *Telephone:*

---

113

# J. M. THEOBALD AND COMPANY'S SPECIALITIES.

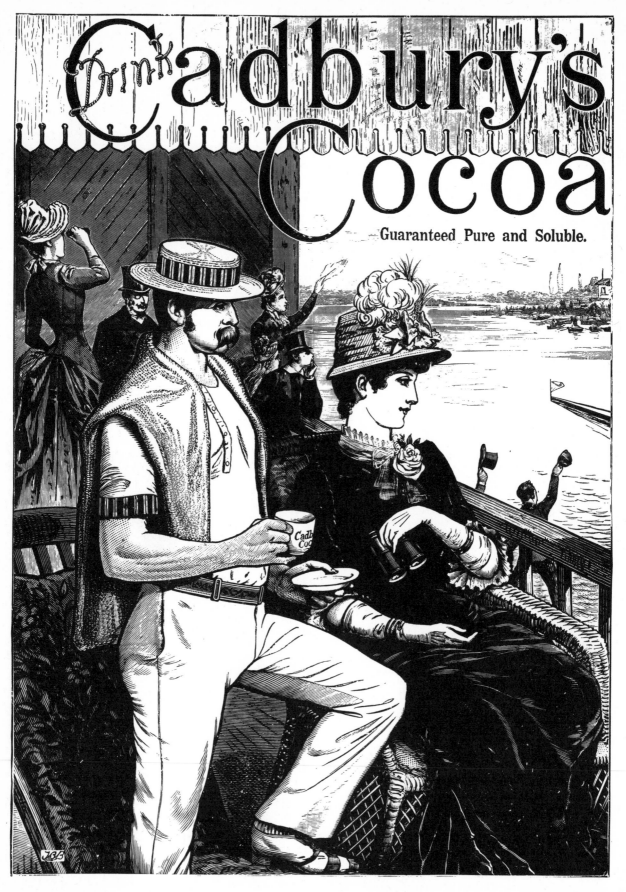

# Drink Cadbury's Cocoa

## Guaranteed Pure and Soluble.

"STRENGTH AND STAYING POWER."—TO ATHLETES.—*The popular beverage for Breakfast, Luncheon, Tea, and Supper, in all seasons, is CADBURY'S COCOA; a pure refined Cocoa—exhilarating, comforting, and sustaining—providing, in a concentrated form, admirable, nutritive, flesh-forming qualities, strength, and staying power. CADBURY'S COCOA is guaranteed absolutely pure, and the public are cautioned to see that they get the genuine article. In the whole process of manufacture, the automatic machinery employed obviates the necessity of its being once touched by human hand. A Sixpenny Packet is sufficient for 14 large Breakfast Cups of strong delicious Cocoa.*

117

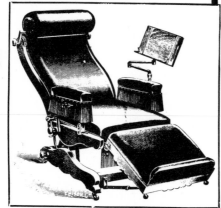

120

## NOTICE.
# CANADIAN CANOES.

ROWLAND WARD and CO., Naturalists, 166, Piccadilly, beg respectfully to inform their numerous Customers who have favoured them with Orders for their HUNTING and FISHING CANADIAN BASSWOOD CANOES, that they have just received the First Shipment, and orders will be executed in rotation. As the supply is limited, to avoid disappointment applications should be sent in before the end of May.

# HART'S
## PATENT THAUMA CARRIAGE.

The Greatest Novelty ever introduced, both simple and useful, particularly adapted for Ladies and Invalids, obviating the necessity of getting over the wheels to obtain their seat. Drawing sent on application. Same price as the ordinary carriage. See opinion of the press.

## 79, NEW BOND-STREET.

"We have had an opportunity of thoroughly examining Mr S. Hart's new invention, applicable to a Stanhope phaeton or waggonette. The idea is a novel one, inasmuch as it enables a lady to enter the vehicle from the back instead of having to climb up over the wheel. In the Stanhope phaeton the back seat is divided in the middle, either side sliding right and left upon the least motion being given; this motion at the same time opens the back portion of the carriage, immediately under which is fixed a flight of steps, which open upon letting down and close upon lifting up. The whole of the machinery is perfectly simple, and in no way interferes with the symmetry of the carriage. The sides of the back seat when opened project over the hind wheels; when shut up the whole fastens with a spring, and is quite imperceptible. The waggonette is if possible more commodious; the same principle being applied, except that the waggonette forms two carriages. It can be used either as a Stanhope phaeton or a waggonette. This is accomplished by removing one of the side seats, and sliding the remaining one into the position which the back seat assumes in the Stanhope. It must also be clearly understood that in both these carriages the front seat moves upon the same action as the back seat, so that upon entering the carriage, the back seat having been opened by a servant, the hand has merely to be placed upon the rail to slide the front seat to the right and left in order to make the required opening, and is closed in the same easy manner. In addition to these very necessary and commodious improvements, the whole of the mechanism of Mr Hart's carriage are light, strong, and beautifully proportioned, whilst their symmetry is as near perfection as possible."—Vide "Court Circular," May 4, 1872.

"The Ladies' Mile."—Once more Hyde Park asserts its ascendancy over the world so far as horseflesh and carriages are concerned. We have long known that nothing could compare with the broughams, the clarences, the phaetons, seen here daily; but with real pleasure we see the patronage accorded to the new patent Thauma Stanhope Phaeton, which gets rid of all the difficulties ladies have had to encounter in getting into a Stanhope or T-cart. Thanks to the patent step and divisional seats invented by Mr S. Hart, 79, New Bond-street, ladies have now no trouble either in entering a phaeton or changing seats while in motion."—Vide "Standard," April 6, 1872.

# ARCHERY.

BOWS, ARROWS, TARGETS, and EQUIPMENTS of the BEST QUALITY at REDUCED PRICES.

An Illustrated Descriptive Catalogue of Summer Games Post Free.

ARCHERY PRIZES.
A Large Assortment of ELEGANCIES IN ORMOLU, &c.
**from 5s. to £10.**
A Parcel of Articles for selection sent on receipt of reference.

ASSER & SHERWIN, 81, Strand, W.C., and 69, Oxford-street, W., London.

# THE "FACILE" BICYCLE
### (BEALE & STRAW'S PATENT)

BICYCLISTS! why risk your limbs and lives on high Machines when for road work a 40in. or 42in. "FACILE" gives all the advantages of the other, together with almost absolut safety. A person of average height may ride a "FACILE" of any size, from 36in. to 42in. The most nervous person may ride the smaller Machine, since the feet are close to the ground, while even with these any reasonable speed may be attained. The action of the feet is vertical, and this gives greater power than the other, as is shown by the ease with which bad hills are mounted. There is no fear of going over the handles, and the powerful Brake may be applied without danger. Intending Purchasers and others are invited to call and inspect the Machine, and wherever practicable, opportunities for Free Trial will be gladly afforded to those who are riders. Descriptive Circular and Testimonials will be sent on application.

SOLE AGENTS:—
# ELLIS & CO.,
(Late of 42, Hart Street, Bloomsbury,)
## 165, FLEET STREET, LONDON.
*(Adjoining Anderton's Hotel.)*

122

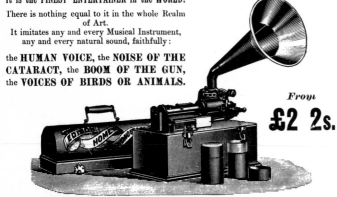

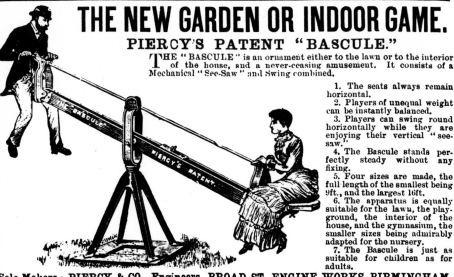

127

# THE GRAMOPHONE,
## OR TALKING MACHINE.

This is an apparatus for reproducing the human voice or other sounds as often as desired; it is intended to be for the voice what photography is for the features. The Gramophone bears no resemblance in a scientific aspect to the Phonograph or Graphophone. Those who have seen and heard it universally pronounce it to be a wonderful Toy.

### Price 2 Guineas.

# PARKINS AND GOTTO,
### 60, OXFORD STREET, LONDON.

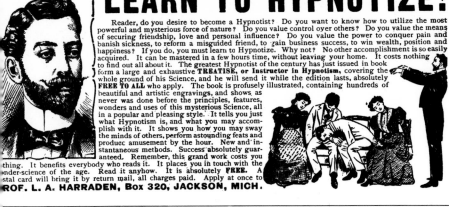

*Prince (loq.): "Try a glass of old Bushmills Whiskey, your Majesty. It is the Whiskey all connoisseurs drink."*

"**BUSHMILLS**" is the purest and most healthful Whiskey produced, being made entirely from the finest procurable Malt, and is never sent out from the distillery until thoroughly matured. Its flavour is unique, partaking partly of the Lowland Scotch and partly of the best-known Irish makes.

All Whiskey drinkers should try "**BUSHMILLS**," which is now recommended by doctors in cases of Gout and Rheumatism as the most healthful drink.

"**BUSHMILLS**" can be obtained at the Army and Navy and other Stores; at the Hotel Metropole, Hotel Victoria, and all the first-class Hotels; at the best Wine Merchants; and at all Spiers and Pond's Buffets. If you have any difficulty in procuring it, write to the London Agent, FRED. J. KING, 3 to 6, CAMOMILE-STREET, E.C.

# THE SHAH AT THE PARIS EXHIBITION.

PRINCE *(loq.)* *This, your Majesty, is the celebrated Bushmills Whisky which you tasted in England, and liked so much.* I feel sure it will get the Gold Medal.

The Prince was right! BUSHMILLS has obtained the *ONLY* GOLD MEDAL.

BUSHMILLS WHISKY is absolutely pure, nothing but the best malted barley being used in the manufacture.

BUSHMILLS WHISKY is very old and thoroughly matured.

BUSHMILLS WHISKY is the most reliable Whisky sold.

BUSHMILLS WHISKY is recommended by medical men.

Can be had in London from THE ARMY AND NAVY CO-OPERATIVE SOCIETY, Limited. 117, Victoria-street, S.W.; at all of SPIERS & POND'S BUFFETS; THE GRAND HOTEL, Trafalgar-square; THE HOTEL METROPOLE, Northumberland-avenue; THE HOTEL VICTORIA, Charing-cross; THE FIRST AVENUE HOTEL, Holborn; THE HOLBORN RESTAURANT; and all leading Wine Merchants throughout the country. London Office and Dépôt—3, 4, 5, and 6, CAMOMILE-STREET, E.C. Birmingham Office and Dépôt—12, COUNTY CHAMBERS, CORPORATION-STREET. Manchester Office and Dépôt—25, HAWORTH BUILDINGS, CROSS-STREET.

Head Offices—1, HILL-STREET, BELFAST. *Established 1704.* Distillery—BUSHMILLS, CO. ANTRIM.

For identification each advertisement is numbered per page in the order of top to bottom in the order of columns from left to right as indicated by this example:

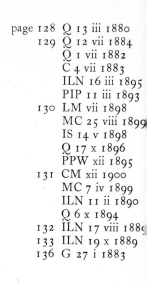

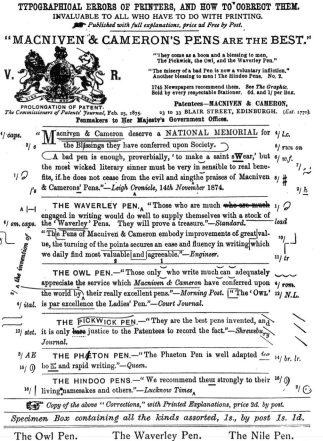